TH.
THE VI...CATION
OF GOD

D. M. Lloyd-Jones

THE BANNER OF TRUTH TRUST

THE BANNER OF TRUTH TRUST
3 Murrayfield Road, Edinburgh EH12 6EL
P.O. Box 621, Carlisle, Pennsylvania 17013, USA

ISBN 0 85151 266 6

Printed by Beshara Press,
Tewkesbury, Gloucestershire.

The Cross

The Vindication of God

D. M. Lloyd-Jones

Whom God hath set forth to be a propitiation through faith in his blood, to declare his righteousness for the remission of sins that are past, through the forbearance of God :
To declare, I say, at this time his righteousness : that he might be just and the justifier of him which believeth in Jesus.

Romans 3. 25, 26

In directing your attention to the great words which are to be found in Paul's Epistle to the Romans in the third chapter, verses 25 and 26, I would remind you again that in many senses there are no more important verses in the whole range and realm of Scripture than these two verses. Here we have the classic statement of the great central doctrine of the Atonement. That is why we are considering it so carefully and so closely. I have said earlier that somebody has described this as the 'acropolis of the Christian faith'. We can be certain that there is nothing that the human mind can ever consider which is in any way as important as these two verses. The history of the Church shows very clearly that they have been the means that God the Holy Spirit has used to bring many a soul from darkness to light, and to give many a poor sinner his first knowledge of salvation and his first assurance of salvation.

Let me give one example and illustration out of history, a well-known and a notable one. I am referring to the poet William Cowper. He tells us that he was in his room in an agony of soul, under deep and terrible conviction. He could not find peace, and he was walking back and fore, almost at the very point of despair, feeling utterly hopeless, not knowing what to do with himself. Suddenly in sheer desperation he sat down on a chair by the window in the room. There was a Bible there, so he picked it up and opened it, and he happened to come to this passage. This is what he tells us: 'The passage which met my eye was the twenty-fifth verse of the third chapter of Romans. On reading it I received immediate power to believe. The rays of the Sun of Righteousness fell on me in all their fulness. I saw the complete sufficiency of the expiation which Christ had wrought for my pardon and entire justification. In an instant I believed and received the peace of the Gospel. If the arm of the Almighty God had not supported me I believe I should have been overwhelmed with gratitude and joy. My eyes filled with tears; transports choked my utterance. I could only look to heaven in silent fear, overflowing with love and wonder.' That is what the twenty-fifth verse of the third chapter of the Epistle to

2

the Romans did for the famous poet, William Cowper. It has done the same thing for many another.

Let me remind you again of what it says. It is a continuation of what the Apostle has been saying in the twenty-fourth verse. It is the great good news that now it is possible for us to be 'justified freely by his grace through the redemption that is in Christ Jesus'. In other words there is a way of salvation now, apart from the Law, which does not depend upon our keeping of the Law. It is this free way which is in Christ. God has ransomed us in Christ and these verses 25 and 26 explain how that ransoming has taken place. But why did it have to happen like that? How does it happen like that?

We have already considered two of the great words which explain this. They are the two great words 'propitiation' and 'blood'. We know also that the redemption purchased in that way comes to us through the instrumentality of faith.

But the Apostle does not stop at that. He says something further. Look at the statement again: 'Whom God hath set forth to be a propitiation through faith in his blood, to declare his righteousness for the remission of sins that are past, through the forbearance of God. To declare, I say, his righteousness at this time, that he might be just and the justifier of him which believeth in Jesus.' Why did the Apostle go on to say all that? Why did he not leave it at that first statement? What is the meaning of this additional statement?

To discover the answer we must consider once more these terms. The first is the term 'set forth'. That means 'to manifest', 'to make plain'. Here is obviously something that is of vital interest to us; it tells us that at once. The death of the Lord Jesus Christ on the Cross on Calvary was not an accident; it was God's work. It was God who 'set him forth' there. How often is the whole glory of the Cross missed when men sentimentalize it away and say, 'Ah, He was too good for the world, He was too pure. His teaching was too wonderful; and cruel men crucified Him!' The result is that we begin to feel sorry for Him, for-getting that He Himself turned on those 'daughters of Jerusalem' that were beginning to feel sorry for Him, and said, 'Weep not for me but weep for your-selves'. If our view of the Cross is one that makes us feel sorry for the Lord Jesus Christ, it just means that we have never seen it truly. It is God who 'set him forth'. It was not an accident, but something deliber-ate. Indeed the Apostle Peter, preaching on the Day of Pentecost, said that it all happened 'by the determinate counsel and foreknowledge of God' [*Acts* 2: 23]. 'GOD hath set him forth.'

The term also emphasizes the public character of the action. It is a great public act of God. God has done something here in public on the stage of world history, in order that it might be seen, and looked at, and recorded once and for ever – the most public action that has ever taken place. God thus publicly 'set him forth as a propitiation through faith in his blood'.

That now brings us to this vital question: Why did God do that? Why did this ever happen? What was it (if I may ask with reverence) that led God ever to do that, that made Him ever purpose to do it? The best answer, still, is to be found by looking at the terms one by one. Then we shall look at them as a whole and we shall see exactly why the Apostle felt that it was so vital and essential to add this to what he has already said.

The first term is this term 'To declare' – 'To declare his righteousness'. This means 'to show', 'to manifest', 'to give an evident token', 'to prove'. God has done this, says Paul, in order that Christ might thus ransom us by giving the propitiatory offering. Yes, but in addition to that, God is 'declaring' something here, He is showing something, manifesting, giving an evident token of something. Of what then? 'Of his righteousness.' We must be careful with this expression, the term we have been looking at since verse 21. It is a little unfortunate that the same term is used to cover two slightly different ideas. So far, as we have looked at this term 'righteousness', we have seen that it means 'a way of righteousness'. Go back to verse 21: 'But now,' he says, 'the righteousness of God without law is manifested.' In other words, 'God's way of making men righteous', 'God's way of giving men righteousness', is what that means. But here it does not mean that. Here he says that God has done something through which He declares His righteousness; not the righteousness which God gives to us, but rather one of God's own glorious attributes. It means God's equity; it means God's judicial righteousness; it means the essential moral, holy, just and righteous character of God. He says again in the next verse (verse 26): 'That he might be just and the justifier of him that hath faith (or believeth) in Jesus' – 'that he might be just'. At the Cross God is declaring His own righteousness, His own righteous character, His own inherent and essential righteousness and justice.

The next word is 'For'. 'To declare his righteousness FOR the remission of sins that are past.' 'For' means 'in respect of', or 'on account of'. He is declaring His righteousness on account of the remission of sins that are past.

The next word is the word 'remission'. Here is a most important word, and it is a pity that the Authorized translation is really most unfortunate at this point. It is one of those cases where the AV is really inferior to the Revised Versions, including the Revised Standard Version, which are right at this point. The AV is an unfortunate translation for this reason. Look up the word 'remission' in your Authorized translation and you will find that it is used a number of times; but if you take the trouble to look up the actual word used in the Greek you will make the very interesting discovery that the word which the Apostle used here, and which is translated 'remission', is only used here in the whole of the New Testament. The Apostle Paul did not use it anywhere else, nobody else used it at all. There is another word which is translated 'remission', and in its various forms you will find it seventeen times in the New Testament; but this word which we have here is only used once, and it really does not mean 'remission'. It means 'pretermission'.

This is an important word and we must look at it. What does 'pretermission' mean? What does 'to pretermit' sins mean as distinct from 'to remit' sins? It is a word that was used in Roman Law. When you find it in Roman Law it is generally used in this sense – it refers to someone who has made a will and who has left somebody out of his will. Imagine a man making a will and leaving something to a number of his friends. But there is one friend to whom he does not leave anything – that is 'pretermission'. He leaves him out of his will; he leaves him out of consideration. It means, if you like, 'to pass over'. That man gave something to all those friends and relatives but he passed over that one – that is to pretermit. That is the very word that is used here – 'to pass over', 'to overlook', 'to disregard', 'to allow to pass without notice', 'to overlook intentionally'. Those are the meanings which were given to this most important word which the Apostle deliberately chose at this point.

Now when the Apostle does a thing like that he must have had a very good reason for it. He does not do that sort of thing accidentally. Why did he not use the word he had used elsewhere? Why this word here, and here only? And why this particular word that means 'passing over'? Clearly because he obviously

7

means to convey the idea of passing over. So instead of translating 'for the remission of sins that are past' we should read, 'for the passing over of sins that are past', 'for the overlooking of sins that are past'. We can put it like this. The difference between 're-mission' and 'pretermission' is the difference between 'forgiving' and 'not punishing'. You may say that that is splitting hairs, that it is a distinction without a difference. But that is not so. Of course, in the end it comes to the same thing. If I do not punish a man, in a sense I have forgiven him; and yet I have not fully done so. If I forgive I certainly have not punished; but to forgive means more than not to punish. So this term 'pretermission', 'passing over', stops short of remission; and that is why it is such a pity that the Authorized Version has 'remission' here. It is 'the passing over', or 'the overlooking of sins that are past'.

The next phrase we come to is this phrase, 'that are past'. 'For the passing over of sins that are past.' Again the Authorized translation is not quite as good as it should be. Taking the AV you might well come to the conclusion that the Apostle is saying that it is the passing over of 'past' sins, anybody's past sins – my past sins, your past sins – 'sins that are past'. But that is not what the Apostle was saying; that is not what he meant. A better translation here would be 'sins that were formerly committed'. He is referring to a very definite time. It is the time which he contrasts in the next verse with 'at this time'. There was *that* time, then *this* time. He says, 'God hath set forth Christ as

8

a propitiation through faith in his blood, to declare his righteousness for the passing over of sins formerly committed, in the forbearance of God; to declare, I say, at this time . . . ' At what is he looking back? He is looking back at the Old Dispensation. He says that God passed over sins under the Old Dispensation, under the old covenant, in the Old Testament times. His point is that God has done that, and has now set forth Christ to do something about what He did then.

That brings us to the last word we have to consider, which is the word 'forbearance'. What is forbearance? Forbearance means 'self-restraint', it means 'tolerance' or 'toleration'. What exactly is the Apostle saying here? 'Whom God hath set forth to be a propitiation through faith in his blood, to declare his righteousness for the passing over of sins formerly committed, through the self-restraint of God.' What does it mean? What Paul is telling us is that this public act which God enacted on Calvary has reference also to God's action under the Old Testament dispensation, when He passed over, when He overlooked, passed by the sins of the people at that time in His self-restraint and His tolerance.

But what does all this mean? In a very interesting way we can answer that question by looking at the same kind of statement in two other places in the New Testament. Do you recall how the Apostle Paul addressed a congregation of Stoics and Epicureans and others at Athens? The account is given in the seventeenth chapter of the book of the Acts of the Apostles, beginning particularly at verse 30. The Apostle, working out his argument, says: 'The time of this ignorance God winked at, but now commandeth all men everywhere to repent.' Observe how he works out his great argument. He says, God has not left Himself without witness through all these generations and centuries. God has left His signs. The object was that people should seek the Lord 'if haply they might feel after him, and find him, though he be not far from every one of us. For in him we live and move and have our being; as certain also of your own poets have said, For we are also his offspring. Forasmuch then as we are the offspring of God, we ought not to think that the Godhead is like unto gold, or silver, or stone, graven by art and man's device. And the times of this ignorance God winked at, but now commandeth all men everywhere to repent: because he hath appointed a day, in the which he will judge the world in righteousness by that man whom he hath ordained; whereof he hath given assurance unto all men, in that he hath raised him from the dead.'

The other passage is verse 15 in the ninth chapter of the Epistle to the Hebrews: 'And for this cause he (Christ) is the mediator of the new testament, that by means of death, for the redemption of the transgressions that were under the first covenant, they which are called might receive the promise of eternal inheritance.' Now that is precisely the same thing. Hebrews 9: 15 says exactly the same thing as the Apostle is saying here. The real commentary then on this verse is found in that statement in Hebrews. That Author was anxious that his readers should be clear about the old covenant and the sacrifices and offerings which the people took to God under the old covenant. They must be quite clear in their minds, and must see quite clearly, that they were never capable of producing a full forgiveness of sins; they did not expiate sin. They could do something, says this man; they were of value in 'the purifying of the flesh'. 'The blood of bulls and of goats, and the ashes of an heifer sprinkling the unclean, sanctifieth to the purifying of the flesh' [*Hebrews* 9: 13]. But they could not do any more. They could not deal with conscience. That is the difficulty. And yet the whole problem is with respect to the conscience. But if the blood of bulls and goats could purify the flesh, 'how much more shall the blood of Christ, who through the eternal Spirit offered himself without spot to God, purge your conscience from dead works to serve the living God?' All that 'was but a figure for the time then present, in which were offered both gifts and sacrifices, that could not make him that did the service perfect, as pertaining to the conscience; which stood only in meats and drinks and divers washings, and carnal ordinances, imposed on them UNTIL the time of reformation. But (now) Christ being come an high priest of good things to come' – and so on.

Do you follow the argument? What he is saying is that under the old covenant, under the Old Dispensation, there was no provision for dealing with sins in a

11

radical sense. It was simply a means, as it were, of passing them by, covering them over for the time being. Those old offerings and sacrifices gave a kind of purification of the flesh, they gave a ceremonial cleanness, they enabled the people to go on praying to God. But there was no sacrifice under the Old Testament that could really deal with sin. All they did was to point forward to this sacrifice that was coming, and that could really do it, and could cleanse the conscience from dead works and truly reconcile man unto God.

Do you mean by that, asks someone, that the saints in the Old Testament were not forgiven? Of course I do not. They were obviously forgiven and they thanked God for the forgiveness. You cannot say for a moment that people like David and Abraham and Isaac and Jacob were not forgiven. Of course they were forgiven. But they were not forgiven because of those sacrifices that were then offered. They were forgiven because they looked to Christ. They did not see this clearly, but they believed the teaching, and they made these offerings by faith. They believed God's Word that He was one day going to provide a sacrifice, and in faith they held to that. It was their faith in Christ that saved them, exactly as it is faith in Christ that saves now. That is the argument.

But that, in a sense, left a problem. The problem was this. God had always revealed Himself as a God who hated sin. He had announced that He would punish sin, and that the punishment of sin was death.

He had announced that He would pour out His wrath upon sin and upon sins. And yet, here was God for centuries, apparently, and to all appearances, going back on His own statements and on His own Word. He does not seem to be punishing sin. He is passing it over. Has God ceased to be concerned about these things? Has God become indifferent to moral evil? How can God thus pass over sin? That is the problem. And it was a very real problem. It is clear that the blood of bulls and of goats, and the ashes of an heifer, cannot do this. And yet God has passed these sins by. How can He do that? What is it that justifies this 'forbearance of God'? Now, says the Apostle, God has really explained it all to us by what He did in public before the whole world, on the stage and in the theatre of the whole world, in Christ on Calvary. He held back His wrath throughout the centuries. He did not disclose it fully then; but He has disclosed it fully now. He has declared it now. Paul says, 'I will repeat that – "To declare, I say" . . . ' That was one of the things that was happening on the Cross. On the Cross on Calvary's hill God was giving a public explanation of what He had been doing throughout the centuries. By so doing, and at the same time, He vindicates His own eternal character of righteousness and of holiness.

How exactly did He do this? Let me answer that question; and as I do so you will see why I was at such great pains to defend that word 'propitiation' and to hold on to it at all costs because it was so vital. How has God done this on Calvary? How has He vindicated His character? How has He given an explanation of His 'passing over' of those sins in past times in His self-restraint and tolerance? There is only one way in which He could do it. God has stated that He hates sin, that He will punish sin, that He will pour out His wrath upon sin, and upon those guilty of sin. Therefore, unless God can prove that He has done that, He is no longer just. What the Apostle is saying is that on Calvary He has done that. He has shown that He still hates sin, that He is going to punish it, that He must punish it, that He will pour out His wrath upon it. How did He show that on Calvary? By doing that very thing. What God did on Calvary was to pour out upon His only begotten and beloved Son His wrath upon sin. The wrath of God that should have come upon you and me because of our sins fell upon Him. God always knew that He was going to do this. We read in the Scriptures of 'the Lamb slain before the foundation of the world'. It was a plan originating in eternity. It was because He knew that He was going to do this that God was able to pass over sins during all those centuries that had gone. Thus, you see, says the Apostle, God at one and the same time remains just and can justify the ungodly that believe in Christ. That was the tremendous problem – how can God remain holy and just, and deal with sin as He says He is going to, and yet forgive the sinner? The answer is to be found alone on Calvary. It is an essential part of what is declared upon the Cross.

That, according to the Apostle, was the first reason.

God had to vindicate what He had been doing in the past under the old covenant. But He had something more to do, he tells us in verse 26: 'To declare, I say, at THIS TIME his righteousness.' He has now explained how He could pass over all those sins in the past. But how does He deal with sin now? How is He going to deal with sins in the future? The answer is still there in the Cross on Calvary's hill. The teaching in other words is this. The Cross on Calvary, the Death of the Lord Jesus Christ, as the Apostle John puts it in his First Epistle chapter 2, verse 2, 'is the propitiation for our sins; and not for ours only but also for the sins of the whole world' – the particular world that is meant there. Sins were dealt with once and for all on the Cross. It is on the Cross that all those sins under the Old Dispensation that God had passed by, and had as it were thus pretermitted – the sins that He had forgiven to Abraham and Isaac and Jacob, and all the believers in the Old Dispensation – it is there the means is provided for doing that. Their sins are included on Calvary. Yes, says Paul, and the sins that are being forgiven now are also dealt with there. And all sins that ever will be committed are also dealt with there.

That is the amazing thing about the Christ of Cavalry – He died 'once and for all'. It is the great argument of the Epistle to the Hebrews, you remember. Those other sacrifices, it says, had to be offered day by day. There was a succession of priests, and they had to go on making their fresh sacrifices. 'But this Man' has made a sacrifice for sins 'once and for ever'. He has dealt with all sins there. There is no need for anything further. There is no need for a fresh sacrifice. It has been done once and for ever. God laid them all on Him there – the sins you have not yet committed have already been dealt with. There, is the means of forgiveness: and there alone. Time past, sins committed formerly, sins committed now, all times – here is the justification of God for forgiving ANY sins whenever committed.

That is what the Apostle is saying here. All sin is forgiven on these grounds, and on these grounds alone. The Cross declares that God 'is just and the justifier of him which believeth in Jesus'. Let me put it in this way. The Cross of Calvary does not merely declare that God forgives us. It does that, thank God, but it does not stop at that. If it only declared that, the Apostle could have finished verse 25 at the word 'blood'. There was no need for more. But he does not stop there, he goes on. He goes on in verse 25 and adds verse 26. Why? Because the Cross is not merely the declaration that God is ready to forgive us.

Another way I can put it is this. The Cross is not merely meant to influence us. But that is what the popular teaching tells us. It says that the trouble with mankind is that it does not know that God is love, it does not know that God has already forgiven everybody. What is the meaning of the Cross? Well, they say, it is God telling us that He has forgiven us; and so, when we see Christ dying, it should break our hearts and bring us to see that. The Cross according to them is directed to us solely. It does speak to us; but it has a grander object than that; it does this other thing also.

Our forgiveness is only one thing; there is something infinitely more important. What is that? It is the character of God. So the Cross goes on to tell me that this is God's way of making forgiveness possible. Forgiveness is not an easy thing for God. I speak with reverence. Why is forgiveness not an easy thing for God? Because God is not only love, God is also just and righteous and holy. He is 'Light, and in him is no darkness at all'. He is as much righteousness and justice as He is love. I do not put these attributes against one another. I say God is all these things together, and you must not leave out the one or the other.

So the Cross does not merely tell us that God forgives, it tells us that that is God's way of making forgiveness possible. It is the way in which we understand how God forgives. I will go further: how can God forgive and still remain God? – that is the question. The Cross is the vindication of God. The Cross is the vindication of the character of God. The Cross not only shows the love of God more gloriously than anything else, it shows His righteousness, His justice, His holiness, and all the glory of His eternal attributes. They are all to be seen shining together there. If you do not see them all you have not seen the Cross. That is why we must totally reject the so-called 'moral influence theory' of the Atonement, the one I have just been describing – the theory which says that all the Cross has to do is to break our hearts and to bring us to see the love of God.

Above and beyond all that, Paul says, He is 'declaring his righteousness for the remission of sins that are past'. Why this, if it is merely a declaration of His love? No, says Paul, it is more than that. If it merely proclaimed His forgiveness we would be entitled to ask whether we can depend on God's word, and whether He is righteous and just. It would be a fair question because God has repeatedly stated in the Old Testament that He hates sin and that He will punish sin, and that the wages of sin is death. The character of God is involved. God is not as men. We think sometimes that it is wonderful for people to say one thing and then do another. The parent says to the child, 'If you do this thing you shall not have that sixpence to buy your sweets'. Then the boy does that thing, but the father says, 'Well, it is all right', and gives him the sixpence. That, we think, is love, and true forgiveness. But God does not behave in that manner. God, if I may so put it, is eternally consistent with Himself. There is never a contradiction. He is 'the Father of lights, with whom is no variableness, neither shadow of turning'. All these glorious attributes are to be seen shining like diamonds in His eternal character. And all of them must be manifest. In the Cross they are all manifested.

How can God be just and justify the ungodly? The

answer is that He can, because He has punished the sins of ungodly sinners in His own Son. He has poured His wrath upon Him. 'He bore our chastisement.' 'By his stripes we are healed.' God has done what He said He would do; He has punished sin. He proclaimed this through the Old Testament everywhere; and He has done what He said He would do. He has shown that He is righteous. He has made a public declaration of it. He is just and can justify, because having punished Another in our stead, He can forgive us freely. And He does so. That is the message of verse 24: 'Being justified (being regarded, declared, pronounced righteous) freely by his grace through the redemption (the ransoming) that is in Christ Jesus; whom God hath set forth as a propitiation through faith in his blood.' Thus He declares His righteousness for having passed over those sins in His time of self-restraint. 'To declare, I say,' His righteousness then, and now, and always, in forgiving sins. Thus He is, at one and the same time, just and the justifier of him that believeth in Jesus.

Such is this great and glorious and wonderful statement. Make sure that your view, your understanding of the Cross, includes the whole of it. Test your view of the Cross. Where does this statement about 'declaring' His righteousness and so on, come into your thinking? Is it something that you just skip over and say: 'Well, I don't know what that means. All I know is, that God is love and that He forgives.' But you should know the meaning of this. This is an essential part of the glorious Gospel. On Calvary God was making a way of salvation so that you and I might be forgiven. But He had to do so in a way that will leave His character inviolate, that will leave His eternal consistency still absolute and unbroken. Once you begin to look at it like that, you see that this is the most tremendous, the most glorious, the most staggering thing in the universe and in the whole of history. God is there declaring what He has done for us. He is declaring at the same time His own eternal greatness and glory, declaring that 'He is light and in him is no darkness at all'. 'When I survey the wondrous Cross . . .', says Isaac Watts, but you do not see the wonder of it until you really do survey it in the light of this great statement of the Apostle. God was declaring publicly once and for ever His eternal justice AND His eternal love. Never separate them, for they belong together in the character of God.

TITLES BY
D. MARTYN LLOYD-JONES
AVAILABLE FROM
THE BANNER OF TRUTH TRUST

ROMANS SERIES:
The Gospel of God (1:1–32)
ISBN 0 85151 467 7, 408 pp.
The Righteous Judgment of God (2:1–3:20)
ISBN 0 85151 545 2, 240 pp.
Atonement and Justification (3:20–4:25)
ISBN 0 85151 034 5, 272 pp.
Assurance (5:1–21)
ISBN 0 85151 050 7, 384 pp.
The New Man (6:1–23)
ISBN 0 85151 158 9, 328 pp.
The Law (7:1–8:4)
ISBN 0 85151 180 5, 372 pp.
The Sons of God (8:5–17)
ISBN 0 85151 207 0, 400 pp.
Final Perseverance (8:17–39)
ISBN 0 85151 231 3, 460 pp.
God's Sovereign Purpose (9:1–33)
ISBN 0 85151 579 7, 344 pp.
Saving Faith (10:1–21)
ISBN 0 85151 737 4, 411 pp.
To God's Glory (11:1–36)
ISBN 0 85151 748 X, 304 pp.

'Dr Lloyd-Jones is a great biblical theologian but the reader will be impressed afresh by the strong experimental note in his theology.'

The Evangelical Quarterly

'It is solid fare that is presented, but with passion and fervour, with simplicity and clarity.'

The Expository Times

'The didactic style that proves so attractive in his pulpit utterances is equally effective in the written page.'

Free Church of Scotland Monthly Record

EPHESIANS SERIES:
God's Ultimate Purpose (1:1–23)
ISBN 0 85151 272 0, 448 pp.
God's Way of Reconciliation (2:1–22)
ISBN 0 85151 299 2, 480 pp.
The Unsearchable Riches of Christ (3:1–21)
ISBN 0 85151 293 3, 320 pp.
Christian Unity (4:1–16)
ISBN 0 85151 312 3, 280 pp.
Darkness and Light (4:17–5:17)
ISBN 0 85151 343 3, 464 pp.
Life in the Spirit (5:18–6:9)
ISBN 0 85151 194 5, 372 pp.
The Christian Warfare (6:10–13)
ISBN 0 85151 243 7, 376 pp.
The Christian Soldier (6:10–20)
ISBN 0 85151 258 5, 368 pp.

(Not available in the USA)

'Characteristically rich in insight, inspiration and interpre-
tation, reflecting his long years of preaching and pastoral
experience . . . Even in printed form these sermons reveal
the authority of the man who preached them and the greater
authority of his message.'

Church of England Newspaper

'Good old-fashioned theological preaching of this kind is a
healthy antidote to the superficiality of many modern
sermons.'

Scottish Journal of Theology

'If you have grown weak on shallow teaching and fuzzy
application, this work will provide strength for the spiritual
muscles and courage for the struggle.'

Moody Monthly

OLD TESTAMENT
EVANGELISTIC SERMONS

ISBN 0 85151 683 1
304 pp. Cloth-bound

'It is vintage wine indeed, and one could have wished for a volume twice the size. Can we expect more?'
Evangelical Presbyterian

'Nearly fifty years on, and the words are in cold print, yet they fire the soul! And surely that is why the book has been published . . . this book may help us to see how a greater mind than ours avoided the distractions and kept to the one great question . . . buy it! You will not be disappointed.'
Evangelical Action

EVANGELISTIC SERMONS
AT ABERAVON

ISBN 0 85151 362 X
308 pp. Large Paperback

'Early examples of that "logic-on-fire" which the author desired and commended to others. To me their abiding value lies in the intense seriousness of the preacher They are worlds apart from the triviality of so much evangelism today.'
Dick Lucas in *The Churchman*

2 PETER

ISBN 0 85151 379 4
272 pp. Cloth-bound;
and
ISBN 0 85151 771 4
272 pp. Paperback

'A masterly example of the kind of expository preaching in popular vein that can result in the building up of a congregation in the Christian faith.'

Reformed Theological Review

'A model for preaching and . . . a storehouse of spiritual benefit.'

Ministry

D. MARTYN LLOYD-JONES:
LETTERS 1919–1981
Selected with Notes by Iain H. Murray

ISBN 0 85151 674 2
270 pp. Cloth-bound

'Take this book reverently, and read to be enriched by the depth of spiritual insight and understanding which God graciously gave to his servant . . . Here is a book well-produced, lovely to handle, full of meaty subjects, with a good photograph of M.L.-J. on the dust-cover . . . it is well worth consideration as a "gift to a friend", but put one on your own shelf first!'

Reformed Theological Journal

AUTHORITY

ISBN 0 85151 386 7
96 pp. Paperback

'These are addresses given at a conference of students in 1957 and are still of superb value for students and young Christians . . . '

Vox Reformata

'This is a splendid introduction to the whole question of authority and may be studied with profit by the specialist or layman alike.'

The Gospel Magazine

WHAT IS AN EVANGELICAL?

ISBN 0 85151 626 2
80 pp. Paperback

'In characteristic style, Dr Lloyd-Jones offers a clear and succinct analysis of the theological trends within Evangelicalism . . . This must surely be one of the most useful books ever to come from Lloyd-Jones.'

Scottish Bulletin of Evangelical Theology

KNOWING THE TIMES
Addresses delivered on Various Occasions
1942–1977

ISBN 0 85151 556 8
400 pp. Cloth-bound

'This is a most significant book . . . a challenge to return to Scripture, to stand by and for the gospel and to live to the glory of God.'

Evangelicals Now

'It ought to be read by every Christian leader. Highly recommended.'

Evangelical Action

'If I had my way, I would make sure that every potential candidate for the ministry not only read this book through, but also read it through regularly, at least once a year . . . probably one of the most significant of all the Lloyd-Jones works that has ever been published . . . it will give both encouragement and vision to those who are concerned with the cause of the gospel.'

The Churchman

THE PURITANS:
THEIR ORIGINS AND SUCCESSORS

ISBN 0 85151 496 0
436 pp. Cloth-bound

'This book is hard to put down; it grips the reader and to it he will want to return again and again. None can read it without immense profit.'

Evangelical Times

GOD'S WAY NOT OURS:
Sermons on Isaiah 1:1–18

ISBN 0 85151 753 6
168 pp. Paperback

'Here is a wonderful example of how to expound the Scriptures without fear or compromise but with a heart of longing for man's salvation.'

Evangelical Times

'Both faithful to the text and powerfully applicable to the present situation . . . [These sermons] were preached in 1963, but reading them you would think they had been delivered last Sunday . . . They show how the prophet's word to Israel can be legitimately applied to the whole human race.'

Foundations

D. MARTYN LLOYD-JONES:
THE FIRST FORTY YEARS

Iain H. Murray

ISBN 0 85151 353 0
412 pp. Cloth-bound, illustrated

In the first volume of the authorized biography of Dr Lloyd-Jones, his story is traced from his rural Welsh background to St Bartholomew's Hospital (where, at the age of 23, he was assistant to Sir Thomas Horder, the King's Physician), then, suddenly, at 27, to a struggling Calvinistic Methodist Mission Church in Aberavon, South Wales. He appears successively as schoolboy, dairyman's assistant, political enthusiast, debater, doctor and finally Christian preacher.

Volume 1 takes us to the start of his ministry at Westminster Chapel, London, on the eve of World War II.

D. MARTYN LLOYD-JONES:
THE FIGHT OF FAITH

Iain H. Murray

ISBN 0 85151 564 9
862 pp. Cloth-bound, illustrated

Volume 2 of the authorized biography takes us through the years of Dr Lloyd-Jones' ministry in London. During this time he also ministered in British universities and in Europe, the United States and South Africa. Ultimately, through his books, he came to exercise a world-wide ministry.

The influence exerted by Dr Lloyd-Jones in so many areas of evangelical life means that this volume is more than the biography of one individual. In many ways it is the story of evangelicalism in the twentieth century.